Yorkshire Landscapes

JO DARKE

Yorkshire Landscapes

B T Batsford Ltd · London

©Opus Books 1983
First published 1983

ISBN 0 7134 4183 6

Typeset by Typewise Limited, Wembley
and printed in Hong Kong

Produced in co-operation with
Opus Books and published by
B. T. Batsford Ltd
4 Fitzhardinge Street
London W1H 0AH

CONTENTS

LIST OF ILLUSTRATIONS

Introduction

You could lose one of England's smaller counties in the former county of Yorkshire, which along part of its western border almost succeeded in stretching from the North Sea to the Irish Sea. The natural boundaries of England's largest county, at least since the ninth century when the Danes divided it into three Ridings ('thriddings') with independent York at the centre, had been the North Sea on the east, the Rivers Tees and Humber on the north and south, and on the west the central section of 'the backbone of England', the Pennines. England's backbone is here displaced, tending westward, and Yorkshire's boundary followed it to capture the highest and most substantial hill country of the central Pennines. Along this westward boundary numerous rivers spring, and they cut west or south-west through deep glaciated 'dales' to reach the soft core of Yorkshire in the Plain of York, a flat swathe cut by Ice-Age glaciers between Yorkshire's northern Jurassic hills and southern chalk wolds, and the Pennine uplands of millstone grit or limestone. Here the western rivers stream southward to gather and flow into the broad Humber.

Over the ages within the confines of these boundaries, have evolved the qualities that make us think of Yorkshire. Scandinavian and Anglo-Saxon place names are everywhere, and observers have noted in the physical appearance and temperament of the people a mixture of Celtic, Scandinavian and Saxon characteristics. Each town or village clinging to the stern cliffs of the northern coast or the crumbling edge of the southern coast has its fishing cobles, whether it is heavily industrialised, picturesque and touristy or a cheerful seaside resort. Medieval monastic orders were attracted to the wild deep river valleys, where they grew rich on wool, and their majestic ruins rise from the valley floors. The wool and textile tradition continued in the south-western dales whose working villages, close to water and then coal, grew to smoky townships under the Industrial Revolution long after the rest of England's great wool industry was forgotten. Powerful medieval families built castles and later fought in the Wars of the Roses and the Civil War, and in the unified England that emerged they created stately homes and spread their influence over vast acreages of countryside. The White Rose of York was adopted as the county emblem, although the wars had nothing to do with differences between Yorkshire and Lancashire, but were between contenders for the English throne whose titles originally had been conferred when the counties of England were shared out among the Norman conquerors. On the lower foothills of the dales, wolds and moors or on the rich agricultural plains grew the tradition of horse breeding, rearing, racing and hunting. Sleepy villages which have sent great Test cricketers from their greens to play in far corners of the former Empire hold in their churches memorials to the Fairfaxes, Scropes, Duncombes, Ingilbys and other influential Yorkshire families along with headstones carrying local names that were associated with a single valley, or perhaps a village, until came the greater mobility, worldwide communication and different expectations of the present age. In general, however, the status quo remains, and the stranger has to be 'wintered, summered and wintered again' before he or she is accepted. Acceptance could be worth waiting for in this spacious country of muted but strong shades: tawny-green or brownish pastures, black hawthorn hedges, walls and buildings of square, deep-grey stone. In spring, daffodils are everywhere and in summer the hawthorn is softened by white or green, while the high black heather moors become a purple sea.

Nowadays the ruined medieval abbeys and castles and the great churches are venerated, and they make up sightseers' itineraries while the mills and warehouses of Victorian times succumb to the bulldozer. The twentieth century has created National Parks and smokeless zones, cleaned the faces of last century's grandiose Town Halls, erected power stations and steel mills and thrown the world's longest single-span suspension bridge across the mile-wide Humber to link the Midlands and northern England along their eastern coasts. Twentieth-century technology is not noted for its contribution to beauty or romance in the landscape but it has performed feats of preservation and restoration, and it is true that one cannot dwell only in the past and that the visual contribution of some

modern architecture need not go unnoticed or unsung. Yet to write about Yorkshire is to deal exclusively with the past, since in terms of official administration Yorkshire has ceased to exist. The demise of this ancient region took place in 1974 when the boundaries of Britain's Economic Planning Regions were redrawn, thereby achieving by pen what had been hitherto impossible by sword. The East Riding now belongs largely to the new county of Humberside, part of which extends along the old Lincolnshire border following the south bank of the Humber. The southern edge of Teesdale, as far east as Darlington, belongs to the new county of Cleveland while corners of the North and East Ridings have moved to the new, all-enveloping county of Cumbria ('Lakeland'), as well as to Durham and Lancashire. These two Ridings are redefined as the Metropolitan Counties of West and South Yorkshire and as the County of North Yorkshire, which now makes England's largest county.

The Gothic majesty of York Minster commands the streets and alleys of the ancient city, still encircled by its thirteenth-century walls.

1 *Through Time to York & the North*

York occupies a low ridge on the Plain, or the Vale, of York, through which people and history have moved since pre-Roman times. Roman roads radiate from the city like spokes of a wheel across the fertile flat land. It was the Romans who first built the plain's major roads, linking their military stations between southern England and the Great Wall. Their route which became known as the Old North Road, now more prosaically called the A1, follows the ribbon of magnesian limestone that forms the gentle folds of the lower Pennines on the western edge of the plain. The Great North Road which runs through York takes a more or less parallel course along the line of the Hambleton Hills which form the plain's north-eastern flank. Along these ancient highways the old coaching towns still provide travellers with welcoming inns, but nowadays the plain is more than a convenient funnel between south and north. Rich undulating farmland, riverside churches, country mansions, once-proud castles or lonely abbey ruins beckon travellers with time to wander and explore.

South of York the plain has fen-like lands bordering the banks of the Humber while ancient towns like Doncaster or Pontefract, lying along the A1, are set at the edge of Yorkshire's industrial heart. Blackened Doncaster, famous for the St Leger, still has its Italianate Grandstand of 1764, and its Mansion House with Corinthian and Ionic columns and Venetian windows built 20 years earlier. Amid a countryside of chimney stacks and cooling towers Arksey, Kirk Sandall, Campsall and other quiet villages hold treasure in their churches and in old buildings grouped along the Don, around village greens or under forest beeches where Robin Hood roamed. Pontefract's grim castle ruin – 'O Pomfret, Pomfret! O thou bloody prison! Fatal and ominous to noble peers!' – stands high above the southern Yorkshire coal measures and above the town's Georgian square and remaining liquorice factories, and the hermitage carved from the living rock that Shakespeare would have known. Off the Great North Road, in Selby's market square, sits one of England's oldest and most complete abbey churches which escaped destruction and was instead bought by the burgesses at Henry VIII's Dissolution because of the harmonious dealings between the monks and the people of this small river port. Although the original noble structure, begun by Hugh de Lacy in 1100, was badly burned in 1906 it was conscientiously restored in the medley of styles it had displayed for centuries. On the outskirts of the town, which still crosses the Ouse with a seventeenth-century timber bridge, are power stations and seed-crushing mills, and the beginnings of coal workings under the surrounding arable and pasture lands. Between Selby and York the countryside provides a more rural setting for villages like Cawood with its great Gatehouse surviving from the Archbishop's Palace where Cardinal Wolsey was arrested, or beautiful Bolton Percy whose church holds memorials to the Fairfax family, or for Bramham Park's magnificent house and gardens designed as a single set-piece and inspired by the French landscape architect le Nôtre, who laid out Versailles; but it is the historic places in their dour industrial surroundings that form our introduction to York and the Plain of York.

York has many facets. For centuries it has been the ecclesiastical, administrative and military capital of the north. It is a river city, and a port; the Ouse and the Fosse are crossed by Victorian

The Ouse, one of the rivers on which York is built, carries cargo barges and pleasure boats while providing the city with over 10 million gallons of water per day.

bridges and the old city is entered by formidable medieval gateways and enclosed by almost uninterrupted medieval walls. The narrow, leaning streets reflect all styles of building from the Middle Ages to the present, with a pleasant predominance of buildings from early or from Georgian times. The beauty and grace of York Minster captures the city's skyline, and sublimely befits York's rôle as head of the northern province of the Church of England. Even the nineteenth-century railway station is a cathedral-like triumph of iron and glass, as satisfying a sight for motorists approaching from the west as for passengers alighting from their trains. The National Railway Museum nearby has the largest collection of railway relics in England, one of many important collections housed in York's formidable selection of museums.

The Roman, Danish, Anglian and Norman eras have left us little to see, but much to contemplate.

The Roman legions made York their headquarters from which to defeat the Brigantes, the warlike British tribe that held all of Northumbria, and Roman Eboracum grew first as a fortress, then as a civilian centre outside the fort, and then as capital of the British Province of the Roman Empire. In 306 AD York saw the death of Constantius Chlorus and the proclamation of his son and successor, later to become Constantine the Great, as Emperor of Rome. York's chief Roman legacy remains in a handsome fragment of the old fortress known as the Multiangular Tower which occupies the grounds of ruined St Mary's Abbey, the Museum Gardens, and also in the extraordinary collection of Roman antiquities which resides with other important archaeological collections in the nearby Yorkshire Museum. The line of the old Roman road, entering Bootham Bar, is continued along Petersgate (where Roman pillars are known to

exist beneath the street) to York Minster, under which can be seen remains of the Roman Praecitium. Christianity was revived here in 627 AD by the baptism of the Anglian King Edwin in a wooden church built within the walls of the Praecitium. The great theologian Alcuin later helped design the stone church that took its place before the city Eoforwic fell to the Danes in the ninth century, and this was replaced in Norman and later times by the gradual growth of the present magnificent Minster of York. Street names ending in 'gate' date from the Danish era, and indeed the Viking city was found recently beneath Coppergate. Conquests by the Saxons and the newly-arrived Normans erased most of the old city, and relics of William's treatment of the rebellious north, which he brutally laid waste, are two castle mounds set up on either side of the Ouse to guard the city against its own people. A quatrefoil keep known as Clifford's Tower, built

in the thirteenth century, survives on the eastward mound. The city's history can be traced from the Middle Ages in buildings like the fourteenth-century Merchant Adventurers' Hall in Fossgate and other fine public or domestic buildings representing every era until the present, and in well-preserved streets like the Shambles – once *Fleshammels*, or 'Street of the Butchers'. St Peter's School, said to be the oldest public school, which was founded by Alcuin (and later attended by Guy Fawkes), is continued in an ornate group of nineteenth-century Gothic buildings, with twentieth-century additions, on the northern side of York. The twentieth century's contribution has been to maintain and augment York's excellent museums and to exercise the astonishing expertise and space-age technology

Kirkgate, the reconstructed Victorian street at York's famous Castle Museum.

that has preserved and restored what is left of medieval York. Some of the most important work was carried out in the 1970s, and the Undercroft Museum shows steel and concrete joists shoring up the foundations of York Minster, with fragments of the Roman Praecitium discovered during the operation. Overhead the mighty Minster soars, the Metropolitan and Cathedral Church of St Peter, the crowning glory of York.

Medieval York must have been dominated by the slow shaping of its great cathedral. Walter de Grey's south transept, built on the earlier Norman structure, emerged between 1220 and 1240 and was followed by the north transept completed in 1260 – both eloquently representing the Early English style. Between 1260 and 1300 the extraordinary octagonal Chapter House appeared in the Decorated style, its vast conical roof, leading outside and timbered inside, supported only by external buttresses. Work

continued on the Decorated nave and choir throughout the fourteenth century, and the twin west towers were completed by 1472, followed by the completion of the lantern tower in 1480. Over these years, stone masons were carving the detail and the decoration shown inside and out – the portrait gallery of tiny heads decorating the canopied stalls in the Chapter House; the delicate pinnacles on the west towers. Over these centuries, too, the unparalleled mastery of York's

Opposite The Heart of Yorkshire: the shape of tracery in York Minster's great West Window earned it this title. One-third of the city's treasury of stained glass is contained in the incomparable windows of the cathedral, and represents craftsmanship from the twelfth to the twentieth century.

Knaresborough and its river, the Nidd, which has cut deep into limestone to create the cliffs on which this fascinating town is built.

14

stained-glass craftsmen was expressed in the grisaille pattern of the thirteenth-century 'Five Sisters' window, slender, pointed lancets in the north transept; the Great West Window dating from 1338, its tracery based on the shape of a heart; the Great East Window of the fifteenth century, its theme the words 'I am the Beginning and the End'; and the Rose Window above the south transept's three lancets, begun in the early sixteenth century to commemorate the marriage of the Lancastrian Henry VII to Elizabeth of York in 1486. The light and beauty of these windows is all the more potent when it is remembered that they represent the combined skills of medieval and twentieth-century craftsmen, for when the glass was removed and safely stored during the Second World War it was dirty and jumbled after centuries of releading or neglect. After the war, local craftsmen took twenty years to reconstruct the true images, employing patience and skill to

match that of the original craftsmen. These images and indeed all of York Minster were spared earlier destruction, it is said, by the admirable Sir Thomas Fairfax who with his family had taken up the Parliamentary cause, and who served as general during the siege of York. Among York Minster's treasures that could have perished is the horn of Ulphus the Saxon whose lands were granted to King Edwin's church and still belong to York Minster, and the Saxon chair in which early Archbishops were throned, both seen in the Chapter House. The little chapel of Archbishop Zouche keeps the only two medieval misericords that survived a fire of 1829 begun by a madman, Jonathan Martin. Here, too, the ancient records of the cathedral are kept. They must reflect the fortunes not only of York Minster but of York, of Yorkshire and the North.

The fortune of Yorkshire and indeed of England was often held in the balance in some of

Fountains Abbey, first founded when this was a wild and inhospitable valley.

Opposite Harrogate is renowned for its superb floral displays – Prospect Gardens and The Prospect Hotel.

15

Studley Royal, the deer park which was created around Fountains Abbey early in the eighteenth century. The classic formality of the park entrance, sustained along the half-mile walk to the abbey, surrounds the medieval magnificence of the ruin.

England's bloodiest battles fought on this flat land around the northern capital. Probably the most fateful was the battle of Stamford Bridge, just east of York, where Harold defeated his brother Tostig and the Norwegian King Harald Hadrada and then was obliged to turn his depleted army south to contend with William of Normandy in Kent. Four centuries later, at the battle of Towton Moor,

> The red rose and the white rose
> In furious battle reeled,
> And yeomen fought like barons,
> And barons died ere yield.

A hillside cross commemorates the site where in 1461, fighting as snow fell, 30,000 men died. On Marston Moor just west of York Prince Rupert suffered a decisive defeat after successfully raising Sir Thomas Fairfax's siege of York, and an impressive obelisk set up by the Cromwellian Association commemorates this battle in which 4000 Royalists and 300 Parliamentarians died.

Lord Fairfax, who was accompanied by his father Fernandino at the Battle of Marston, was often followed on the battlefield by his wife Mary, and even by his infant daughter, riding with a maid. After the war, the family lived at Nun Appleton Hall where Sir Thomas wrote his books and shared inspiration with his daughter's tutor Andrew Marvell, born in Holderness. Here Marvell produced some of his best poems, and dedicated to Lord Fairfax a ballad which tells of an ancestral romance. The poem speaks with affection of the Fairfax family and their estates:

> Then, languishing with ease, I toss
> On Pallets swoln of Velvet Moss;
> While the Wind, cooling through the Boughs,
> Flatters with Air my panting Brows.

This image of rural solitude can be experienced still in many villages, grand houses, castles or churches which follow the main roads and their market towns, watered by the many rivers or their tributaries, along the Plain of York. Typical is the village of Nun Monkton with its green, maypole, brick cottages, sixteenth-century Hall thought to occupy the site of a Benedictine nunnery, and church obscured by a weeping beech at the end of a tree-lined avenue.

Knaresborough has an old-world charm entirely of its own. Like nineteenth century Harrogate nearby the town stands at the western edge of the plain, on the limestone foothills of the lower Pennines. It is an ancient place, haphazardly mounting steep crags and slopes on one side of a gorge cut by the River Nidd, and its somewhat bloodthirsty past is associated mostly with its castle which is now a ruin but of which in the sixteenth-century John Leland wrote, 'The castle standith magnificently and strongly as a Rok'. From here there is a fine view of gorge, river and town, and of the railway viaduct about which Sir Nikolaus Pevsner coldly remarked, 'To castellate the bridge does not make it a picturesque object'. Near the castle in Knaresborough's handsome market place one of the period buildings claims to be the oldest chemist's shop in England. Between the market place and the river the most intriguing of the many interesting buildings are the various caves, one a hermit's chapel and one his dwelling, carved out of the living rock. Mother Shipton's cave, too, can be seen, although her prophecies of the sixteenth century need not necessarily be believed, while an indisputably real marvel across the river is the Dropping Well where personal objects hung beneath water dripping over a ledge are petrified by its limestone content. In St John's Parish Church with its pretty spirelet are monuments of the Slingsby family, among them William Slingsby, his image now leaning pensively in an arched niche, who discovered another natural phenomenon when in 1571 he recognised the sulphurous taste of waters in the neighbouring Tewit Well as having properties similar to medicinal waters he had tasted in the Belgian town of Spa. Thereafter grew Harrogate.

Until the Duchy of Lancaster began to develop the place as a spa in 1840, Harrogate consisted of one or two inns and some embryonic terraces. Today, as a nineteenth-century resort that has not suffered too much twentieth-century development, it is elegantly fitted for its recently adopted rôle as a conference town. The approach from Sheffield or Leeds is punctuated by expansive acreages of grass, ringed with Victorian villas, that lead right into this spacious, hilly town. These are known as the strays, and cover 200 acres of land that were set aside to allow access to the many outlets of medicinal waters discovered after William Slingsby's original find. On one stands the parish church. Much of Harrogate's charm derives from its seeming to have grown rather than to have been planned, while it looks well cared-for and has many lovely gardens which make a bright foil for its magnificent hotels, teashops and villas built of dark stone and embellished with Victorian iron and glass. The

The nave of Ripon Cathedral: a trapdoor in the choir leads to the seventh-century crypt of St Wilfrid.

Royal Baths, now the Royal Baths Assembly Rooms, stand in their Valley Gardens which were once known as Bogs Fields. To appreciate the rich tiling and bathroom furniture of the original Victorian temple to health, you must indulge in a Turkish bath – the only part of the original complex that still serves the same purpose. To appreciate the charm of Harrogate, it is best to meander with the streets and come across such features as the tea rooms and toffee shops (Harrogate's famous toffee was developed, perhaps, as an antidote to too much health), the first spa waters of the Tewit Well, now encompassed by Tuscan columns and a dome, and the well-known Harlow Car Gardens 'the Wisley of the North' – the Royal Horticultural Society's testing-place for plants.

From unhistorical Harrogate, the march of history follows in the footsteps of England's first great road builder John Metcalfe, known as Blind Jack of Knaresborough. Disabled through smallpox at the age of six, he grew to pursue a varied and exciting career in which one of his achievements was to establish techniques for laying routes over boggy country. Under the Turnpike Acts of the eighteenth century he was responsible for repairing or rebuilding many of England's roads, one of them from Harrogate through Knaresborough to Boroughbridge. A little way from the cobbled market place and red-roofed houses of this old coaching town stand the Bronze-Age Devil's Arrows, Yorkshire's best known prehistoric site. These standing stones of millstone grit were described by Edward Baines in 1821 as 'stupendous obelisks called *the arrows*, of an irregular form, though somewhat pyramidical and worn by exposure to the weather into channels at the top, which makes them appear as if fluted'. By Baines's time there were three stones; one had been used in Blind Jack's Peggy Bridge over the River Tutt. Part of this great stone can be seen a little way south at Aldborough, which was a much more important place until the Ure was bridged by the Normans at Boroughbridge. Formerly the Brigantian capital Iseur and later the northern headquarters of the ninth Roman legion, Aldborough today with its green and maypole is a sleepy village embellished with Roman remains, which are mostly deposited in the museum. Isarium Brigantium's city wall survives, and some of its stones became part of Aldborough's fine fifteenth-century church which among its furnishings and ornaments has a panel of

Mercury built into the west wall of the north aisle.

Roman, or Roman-styled, statuary is to be found in a formal and grand setting at Newby Hall, whose herbaceous borders and rock gardens slope down to the River Ure three or four miles up-river from Aldborough and Boroughbridge. The mansion was begun early in the eighteenth-century for Sir Edward Blackett, whose wealth grew from the coal-mining industry. Later that century the building was transformed to express the mastery of Robert Adam, who drew round him a team with skills to match his own so that the ceilings by Zucchi, Gobelin tapestries by Boucher and Neilson and furniture by Thomas Chippendale, who was Yorkshire born, would become an integral part of Adam's structural design and ornamentation. This exquisite interior was conceived as a setting for the collection of sculpture brought back from a Grand Tour of Italy by the Hall's owner, William Weddell, and the result in all its rich harmony makes one of the finest interiors in the country.

Another glorious interior can only be imagined at Fountains Abbey whose remains stand in the classically-landscaped park at Studley Royal, west of Newby Hall. It is hard to believe that the formal lawns, the waterside temple, the well-tended shrubberies which now line the deep wooded valley of the Skell were in the twelfth century a place remote from all the world, uninhabited, set with thorns...' a wilderness chosen deliberately by monks dissatisfied with the lax system at St Mary's Abbey in York, who preferred to emulate the Cistercian philosophy of hard work and Spartan living in unsympathetic country. By the time of the Dissolution, hard work, wool and generous endowments had made this the richest abbey in the land. So Henry found it; so he sold it, and in the late eighteenth century William Aislabie acquired it and integrated the romantic ruin with his adjoining estate of Studley Royal. Today, its grounds and beautiful rose-pink stone are well-cared for by the Department of the Environment. It is the best-preserved and most complete of all the English abbeys and was completed by the mid-thirteenth century, but for Archbishop Huby's north tower which was added just before the Dissolution. Visually most striking are the lofty grace of the Chapel of the Nine Altars, which forms an east transept, and the immense vaulted cellarium with its double row of arches extending 100 yards to the river. The great east window of the church and the arcading in the

Gentle countryside of Sutton Bank: the White Horse of Kilburn, carved into the oolitic limestone of Whitestonecliffe, stands out above the villages of Kilburn and Coxwold.

nave remind us of the dominating and disciplining force in the monks' lives. Details like the stone coffin in the presbytery, the towel cupboard next to the warming house – the only part of the abbey that was heated – or the inscribed bands on Archbishop Huby's tower, with decorative shields and the statue there, fill the draughty walls with ghosts.

Very much alive are the office and duties of the horn-blower at Ripon, one of the most important coaching towns along the Old North Road. For centuries every evening at nine o'clock in Ripon's market place the horn-blower in a tricorn hat has sounded the Wakeman's horn. The oldest building in the square with its old and welcoming inns is the timber-framed Wakeman's House, now an information centre and folk museum, and the grandest building is the Town Hall displaying large gilt letters on a maroon background: *Except ye Lord keep ye cittie, the Wakeman waketh in vain.* By the time the Town Hall was built by James Wyatt in 1801 these words were outdated, for the Wakemen – or watchmen – had been replaced early in the seventeenth century by mayors. An ancient survival is the Saxon crypt of St Wilfrid's church which now forms part of Ripon Cathedral with its great gabled and turreted west front. Inside the church are fanciful images by the well-known Ripon woodcarvers, while monuments include that of Ripon's last Wakeman and first mayor, Hugh Ripley; members of the Aislabie family; Margaret Lupton whose children and grand-children were reputed to number around 150; and members of the Markenfield family whose moated, fortified manor is now incorporated into a farm and stands in all its medieval simplicity deep in the countryside three miles south.

Travellers following a circuitous course along and around the Old North Road will come across places whose significance has grown or declined during different periods, mostly in the time since the Romans constructed and marched along this route. The Great North Road from York follows an equally enticing course, passing alongside the great scarp of the Hambleton Hills where Sutton Bank affords stupendous views – and gliding facilities – across the patchwork plain. Villages nestle beneath, like Laurence Sterne's Coxwold: 'O tis a delicious retreat!', or nearby Kilburn whose schoolmaster and his pupils carved out the great White Horse on Roulston Scar, 600 feet above, in 1857. The distinguished woodcarver Robert Thompson, Yorkshire's 'mouse man', was born in Kilburn 19 years later, and established the oak-carving workshops that are the village's main industry. Between Coxwold and Kilburn, and lost in the undulating countryside, is the striking ruin of Byland Abbey with its rose window reduced to a ghostly half-circle, a shadow of what was once one of the biggest Cistercian houses in its time. No doubt the monks, and those from nearby Rievaulx, took advantage of the Roman road and the medieval market towns: Easingwold, then Thirsk with its fine church; Northallerton, formerly the capital of the old North Riding and now administrative centre for North Yorkshire. From here the roads run north across Teesdale to Durham, or north-east to Middlesborough which was Yorkshire's 'boom town' of the last century. Today Middlesborough lies at the heart of the industrial complex around Teesside which was once shared by Yorkshire and County Durham, but now forms the heart of a new county, Cleveland. This industrial county is well named, for it owes its existence to the ironstone that was discovered in 1850 and mined along the Teesdale face of Yorkshire's Cleveland Hills, the northern limit of today's North York Moors National Park.

The gaunt remains of Byland Abbey, near Coxwold, still retain remnants of green- and yellow-tiled floors. A former abbey was begun further north on a site now known as Old Byland, but the Cistercian monks moved because Rievaulx Abbey stood in a nearby valley and each could hear the other's bells – 'which was not fitting and could by no means be endured'.

2 Over the Lonely Moors

The North York Moors National Park gathers under its administrative wing the moor and hill, river and beck, dale, vale and sea coast which form the north-east corner of Yorkshire and centre around the North York Moors. These silent and lonely heights, sombre with heather until summer's purple bloom, form a ridge that runs eastward from the Cleveland Hills to the sea. The Cleveland Hills wriggle round in an outer arm, making a northern and western edge, separated from the moorland ridge by the Esk valley which cuts eastward to Whitby, fed by becks from the hills. The Hambleton Hills, continuing the southward trend of the Cleveland Hills, form a barrier between the Plain of York and the series of deep dales that run southward from the moorland ridge to create an extensive river system draining into the flat damp grassy Vale of Pickering where the river Derwent flows. The high moorland ridge is characterised by spurs, called riggs, that divide the dales. The dales, long steep river valleys of heather and bracken, pastured by sheep, offer some of Yorkshire's most peaceful scenes. The loneliest are on the moors themselves, their great tracts of heather and bracken black or dark brown for much of the year in which, the local saying goes, 'There's eight months of winter and four months of cold weather'.

It is across these exposed lands, where scenery is created as much by the intangible play of light and shade as by the terrain, that the Lyke Wake walkers go. Their route is intended to traverse the highest and loneliest part of the North York Moors and indeed of Yorkshire, and it covers 40 heathery, boggy miles between the Plain of York and the sea. Its name is taken from the Lyke Wake Dirge, a remnant of the ancient custom of 'waking', or keeping vigil, over a dead body – a *lyke* – to prevent the Devil from stealing the soul before burial. The starting point for the walk is close to Osmotherley and to the nearby ruin of Mount Grace Priory which stands sequestered under steep woods of Ingleby Moor, its rough grassland golden with daffodils in spring and buttercups in summer. Founded in 1398, this is England's best-preserved example of a Carthusian monastery and the only one surviving in Yorkshire. After the Dissolution, Mount Grace fell into lay hands, and enough remains to give a vivid picture of the hermetic lives of the monks who occupied single two-storey cells with their own workshops and walled gardens. Meals were passed through a dog-leg hatch, and the monks met only to pray, or on special occasions. This ancient site will be one of many encountered along the walkers' route, which crosses close to heads of dales running southward to the Vale of Pickering – Bilsdale, Farndale, Rosedale – and those feeding the Esk to the north. The route passes disused ironstone mines on Rosedale Moor, and follows jet miners' or ancient packhorse tracks. Waymarks come in the form of crosses or carved stones such as the carved 'Face Stone' that has a Celtic look on Urra Moor, or the Rud Stone which stands close to the paved causeway known as 'Smugglers' Trod', or Ralph's Cross on Rosedale Head, where wayfarers once left alms for needy travellers. All along the route are the burial mounds, or 'howes', of the Celtic tribes, contrasting strangely with the image of the whitish round radomes of the Ministry of Defence's Early Warning System on Fylingdales Moor, possibly as unnerving as any bargest, gabbleratchet or other fearsome entity that in legend roamed the moors after dark.

The route passes the beautiful North Yorkshire Moors Railway which travels from Whitby via Grosmont and Goathland through Newtondale, past Levisham to Pickering. It may well be tempting for walkers to abandon the project at this point, and spend some time exploring places like Goathland, where sheep nibble the broad village green, or the wild moors around the sleepy village of Levisham. At the head of Levisham Beck is the famous Hole of Horcum, a vast depression which was once farmed at the bottom but now is haunted by hang-gliders. The North York Moors National Park's relatively small area is appreciated by a wide range of visitors, from those who wish to tangle with wind and weather on the ghostly moor, or to glide, or to fish or swim on the coast, to those who prefer 'just looking' – whether on foot or on wheels. From Levisham station people who prefer wheels can take a train on the railway – a scenic route now run by a voluntary trust – and travel north across the moors to Whitby, or south along Newtondale to Pickering and the Vale of Pickering.

The scooping, sculpting Ice-Age glaciers heaped up boulder clay against the Scandinavian ice sheet along the east coast from Scarborough to Filey. In prehistoric times this formed a lake whose waters were held between the northern moorland foothills and the chalk wolds and, on the western edge, by the gentle Howardian Hills. The bed of the lake is flat damp farmland, and along its northern edge are the villages and deep dales which make some of the loveliest countryside in Yorkshire, where rivers and becks pour down through heather and trees, threading between stone houses of villages, to meet the River Derwent. The present source of the Derwent is in the eastern moors, but its waters are prevented from entering the sea by the glacial

Fertile farmland softens the windswept uplands of the North York Moors at Glaisdale, within sight of the coast around Staithes.

For centuries, sheep have grazed the bleak pastures of the North York Moors. Here they nibble unperturbed around the radomes of the Fylingdales Early Warning system, set up in 1961.

ridge and so it is forced to reverse its original route and to amble across the Vale. It breaches the Howardian Hills at the former Roman station and present market town of Malton, gateway to the Vale, and then at Kirkham Priory where the river turns southward to flow along the Plain of York. The National Park contains all the villages and dales watered by the Derwent's many tributaries which form the northern fringe of the Vale where each vista of rock and river and trees, each drowsy village green or shaded church, is as enticing as the next. Some hold unexpected treasure.

Overlooked by its castle ruin, the ancient town of Pickering is a hilly huddle of red-roofed houses gathered around a stately church whose steeple makes a landmark in the Vale. Under the whitewash in the church, in 1851, some of England's finest medieval wall paintings were uncovered and quickly whitewashed again by the

vicar who felt the images 'have a tendency to excite feelings of curiosity and distract the attention of the congregation'. Later cleaned and restored, the pictures have lost none of their vitality. St Christopher climbing from the tossing river glances reassuringly at the Christ child on his shoulder, St George triumphs over the dragon, Salome presents Herodias with St John's head on a plate, and the figures of Adam and Eve emerge from the dragon-jaws of Hades to be greeted by Christ who has descended into Hell after his crucifixion.

Other treasures to be explored might lead you from the picturesque village of Thornton-le-Dale along the Sneverdale Forest Trail or, at the village church of Lastingham north-west of Pickering, down among the carved rams' heads on the sturdy pillars of the crypt which was built in 1078 by the Abbot of Whitby, Stephen, as a repository for the bones of St Cedd who founded a

monastery here. Nearby at the Ryedale Folk Museum in Hutton-le-Hole, a weathered village within sight of the moors, you can see fine displays based on local crafts as well as carved posts that were used until well into the last century as protection against witchcraft. To either side of these villages are Rosedale, watered by the River Seven, and Farndale with its famous tide of springtime daffodils waving among fields and trees for nine miles along the banks of the Dove. At the village of Gillamoor, high above the dale, visitors can delight in the 'surprise view' which appears at a turn in the road leading to the church. At the foot of Farndale, close to Kirkbymoorside, is the village of Kirkdale where an Anglo-Saxon sundial has passed the time sheltered by the porch of the church which has preserved its inscription carved in Old English: 'Orm, the son of Gamal, bought St Gregory's minister when it was all broken down and fallen

and he caused it to be made new from the ground, to Christ and St Gregory in Edward's days the King in Tosti's days the earl'. The sundial occupies the centre of a slab seven feet long and two feet deep, and measures the eight hours of the Saxon day. Near the village, in 1821, a cave was discovered to contain the bones of men and hyenas and the flints of Mesolithic hunters, whose days perhaps were counted in terms of sunset and sunrise.

The days of the Cistercian monks at Rievaulx Abbey in Ryedale were passed in work and prayer. Their lives can be traced from the ground plan of what is perhaps the most romantic ruin in Yorkshire, set in a valley so narrow that the prescribed east-west orientation had to be ignored by the builders. The twelfth-century work shows the severe style approved by the order while thirteenth-century building, particularly that in the presbytery, shows the

relaxing of this rule in the tiers of arcading and lancet windows, and the dogtooth decoration of clerestory and triforium. The resulting harmony in stone, even ruined stone, leaves an example of some of our finest Early English architecture. Rievaulx was the first substantial Cistercian house in Yorkshire and founded many daughter abbeys, achieving such power and wealth from sheep farming that the third abbot Aeldred's biographer Walter Daniel, a monk at Rievaulx, likened the abbey with its 140 monks and over 500 lay brothers to 'a hive of bees'. By the Dissolution the abbeys had long been in decline, largely because the Black Death had drastically reduced the numbers of lay brothers on whom the abbeys were dependent for labour, and Rievaulx by then supported only 22 monks in a building already falling into disrepair. Today's homely stone cottages that stand in the same valley add a human touch as they appear framed in the skeletal arches of this once-great abbey. For drama and romance nothing can compare with the views afforded through a veil of trees from high up along formal terraced gardens winding above the valley's rim.

The terrace is embellished at either end with an elaborate Grecian temple, and it was laid out in 1758 by Sir Thomas Duncombe. It forms part of a fine park occupying the grounds of Helmsley's gaunt ruined castle battered in the Civil War by Lord Fairfax and patched up by Fairfax's later son-in-law the Duke of Buckingham as his final retreat, only to be acquired by the wealthy banker Sir Charles Duncombe after Buckingham died destitute in 1687:

And Helmsley, once proud Buckingham's delight,
Slid to a scrivener, and a City Knight.

Pope's 'scrivener', whose ancestors still own the castle ruin, laid out the park and built a grand mansion which is now a girls' school. Altered by Barry in 1848 it was designed in 1713 by William Wakefield, the squire of Huby Hall in Easingwold, and it has even been attributed to Vanbrugh. Perhaps this is not surprising since this personable dramatist-turned-architect's first creation was the vast mansion Castle Howard, which rises nearby amid the low contours of the Howardian Hills. In 1700, with Wren's pupil Nicholas Hawksmoor as Clerk of Works, Vanbrugh began the wildly innovative and immense manion on a site provided by demolishing a village. Despite this cavalier attitude of former times it is impossible not to marvel at the scale and proportions in Castle Howard's great blocks of varying heights with their rows of windows united under a central dome, or at the stately marble hall which opens on to a series of long corridors holding a treasury of furniture and painting, or at the extensive parks and gardens with Vanbrugh's Gatehouse and Temple of the Four Winds and with Hawksmoor's Mausoleum, and with lakes and statuary fit for kings.

Helmsley's red roofs, rushing river, old inns, generous market square and ruined castle make a good starting – or finishing – point for the Countryside Commission's 100-mile footpath the Cleveland Way, which embraces the northern half-circle of the National Park from here to Filey Brigg, North Yorkshire's southernmost coastal resort. Conceived in the 1930s, the route was opened at Helmsley Castle in 1969, 14 years after the unofficial Lyke Wake Walk. The two routes meet after the Cleveland Way has followed in the footsteps of pre-Roman tribes along the Hambleton drove road from Kilburn to Osmotherley, where John Wesley preached on a great stone slab that still stands by the village cross. They converge for 12 miles and have much in common, particularly in the predominance of prehistoric sites and of Norse place names; of heather, and bog. They cross the main heights of the Cleveland Hills, a series of plateaux, the familiar outlines of Carlton Bank, Cringle Moor, Cold Moor and Hasty Bank (from the Norse *hestas*, a horse). The Cleveland Way is more varied, passing through forest and farms and close to villages or towns along the edge of the Cleveland Hills where walkers can be put up for the night. Stokesley, a small market town by the River Leven, is a beguiling place with cobbled alleys and bridges, and a long market place. Ingleby Greenhow's village church which was rebuilt in the eighteenth century has some fine Norman work, and the village is close to Easby Moor a few miles north, whose 1064-foot summit is crowned by the monument to Captain Cook: 'A man in nautical knowledge inferior to none, in zeal, prudence and energy superior to most'. Even more dramatic is Roseberry Topping, a hill which derives its name from the Vikings' *Odinsberg*. These invaders may have been among the many peoples who mined the hills for iron stone, alum and jet, while staying close to the familiar North Sea. Reaching the coast at Saltburn, walkers turn south-east and follow the towering cliffs and fantastic industrial seascapes

Chugging uphill between Goathland and Grosmont on the North Yorkshire Moors Railway, built in 1836. After closure by British Rail, the line was reopened by enthusiasts and now operates as a popular mode of travel for sightseers.

Thornton-le-Dale, prettiest in a string of picture-postcard villages along the Vale of Pickering at the southern edge of the North York Moors.

of Skinningrove and Boulby, where they are likely to experience the full force of the winds that come howling across the moors, straight from the North Sea. A pleasant stopping-place is the first of North Yorkshire's steep fishing towns, Staithes.

This fascinating place looks as it might when the Reverend John Graves, writing his *History of Cleveland* in 1808, described Staithes as 'singularly situated in a narrow creek between two cliffs, and so near the shore, that the sea reaches many of the houses at high water'. This closed-off community has only comparatively recently shed its pure – and incomprehensible – Cleveland coastal dialect, and the women's 'Staithes bonnets' were a familiar sight until well into the present century. Like most other coastal settlements along here, Staithes prospered from fishing in the nineteenth century and from smuggling in the eighteenth. Captain Cook's

apprenticeship was served in a haberdashery which has since been washed away, from which he is said to have run away to Whitby, carrying a clean shirt and a knife, to sign on as 'servant' in the collier *Freelove*. Dame Laura Knight lived and painted here; the town's population today works the fishing cobles, or in the industrial towns further north along the coast, which gives Staithes the homely feel of a lived-in town.

Whitby, too, has the slightly run-down charm of a working town with a history. It spreads along either side of the Esk as the broad river, after forging its way through Eskdale and the moors, here enters the sea. The river is crossed by through traffic over a high-level bridge opened in 1980 which by-passes the town, while the handsome swing-bridge of 1902 links east and west Whitby. The views across water busy with fishing boats and wheeling gulls to either side of the crowded town are equally rewarding. The old

town nestles under the steep western cliffs which are crowned by Whitby's ancient landmark, its ruined abbey. In all parts are corners worthy of exploration, some well-known like Captain Cook's house in Grape Lane or the Town Hall, and others – steps cut into the cliffs, narrow alleys or cobbled yards – which add to the sense of history in this old sea port. Jet workings can still be seen in the coastal cliff face, and pieces picked up off the shore, although the days of Whitby's pre-eminence are gone. The Brigantes, Romans, Saxons, Danes and Normans all knew and used Whitby jet, which in the Victorian era brought fresh industry to Whitby as the whale fisheries declined. Memories of Whitby's greatest industry, the whale fisheries, come from the handsome Georgian houses – Captains' houses – still to be seen in the town. In those days the name of Captain Scoresby was equal, locally, to that of Captain Cook. Scoresby's whalers, made more manoeuvrable than others, ventured further north than any of their fellows and during Whitby's zenith in the late eighteenth century made 30 journeys to the fishing grounds around Newfoundland and the Arctic, to bring back a total of 533 whales. Cook meanwhile was leading the Royal Society's expedition to find a 'Great Southern Continent' aboard a refitted Whitby collier. Renamed *Endeavour*, the ship sailed from Plymouth in 1768 and returned in 1771 having circled New Zealand, explored the east coast of Australia, and circumnavigated the world.

The lives of early Christian missionaries, who left such an imprint on this region, might have seemed as colourful and bizarre to men like Scoresby and Cook as their own adventures seem to us in these days of armchair travel. More than a thousand years before Cook's meetings with Australian Aboriginals who, as he reported, went 'Naked and not ashamed', King Oswy had vowed

A classic view of Rievaulx Abbey in its narrow valley which is the most romantically sited of Yorkshire's great Cistercian houses.

Overleaf Ancient walls of Rievaulx Abbey. The church buildings have a north-south orientation, dictated by the narrowness and the westward slope of the valley.

31

Opposite Vanbrugh's first masterpiece, Castle Howard. This vast and imposing palace has been occupied by members of the same family who commissioned its design.

The pinnacled church tower at Helmsley, on the River Rye, a pretty market town which marks the western end of the Cleveland Way.

Huddled under the protective arm of the Nab, and with the wild moors behind, Staithes is a picturesque and unspoiled coastal town, once the most important fishing centre on the North Yorkshire coast.

to found 12 monastic houses, and to dedicate his infant daughter in chastity to the monastic life, if he were granted success in overcoming the pagan king Pendra. Whitby Abbey was one of six in *Deira* (Yorkshire) duly founded by the king whose daughter, Aelfled, succeeded the first abbess Hilda in AD 680. Jointly occupied by men and women, the abbey achieved renown as a centre of learning and the home of the poet-monk Caedmon whose writing so moved Bede and his contemporaries. The most important recorded event in the early abbey's existence, also chronicled by Bede, was the Synod of Whitby of 664 at which it was decided that the Roman ritual, including the celebration date of Easter, should prevail over that of the Celtic church. After Bede's death the abbey's history went largely unrecorded, and in the ninth century it was obliterated by the pagan Danes. The present haunting ruin of the abbey church, set starkly on the clifftop rather than in the shelter of a hill or dale, dates from the twelfth to the fourteenth centuries, and has been a gaunt landmark to homecoming sailors for centuries.

North Yorkshire's coastal villages or towns are linked by a motor road that rolls over the moors a mile or so inland through dark heather which stretches from horizon to horizon with here and there a bent pine tree. Rough pastures are bounded by square-cut hawthorn strips, and black-faced sheep graze the fields. Side roads stretch across this bleak moorland to the high cliffs and the sea, whose erosive action makes the layered shales, clays and sandstones disconcertingly unstable. The ancient past is discernible in remains of Roman signal stations which formed part of the legions' defence of the Saxon Shore, while the Vikings' contributions include place names, dialect, and perhaps the fishing cobles themselves. The wind, waves and the sea fogs – known locally as sea frets – have left their legacy of shipwrecks, and unforgotten stories of heroism in saving lives from the furious sea.

One of the most picturesque of the old fishing towns is Bay Town of Robin Hood's Bay which clings tenuously to the steep cliffs at the northern end of this fossil-rich arc. The headlands that hold the curve are called North Cheek and South Cheek, which gives the impression of a broad

smile on an otherwise frowning coastline. For cliff walkers, the views across the bay from North Cheek to the 600-foot cliffs at Ravenscar are grand, and the sudden steep descent down the one-in-three slope between the red roofs of Bay Town is – literally – breathtaking. Like Whitby, this rather Dickensian place with its sizeable holiday population was involved in the whaling trade, and behind the tall narrow cottages in the main streets are the handsome eighteenth-century mansions of the whaling captains. The author Leo Walmsley lived in an Elizabethan house, and the village embraced in the arm of the bay has attracted many artists. A small stream gushing in from the moorlands runs under the houses, while the sea will sometimes rush up the streets, and once drove a ship before it until the bowsprit became lodged in the window of an inn. The floor of the bay here is composed of massive black slabs that form part of an eroded dome, the foundations of softer cliffs which are wearing away at the rate of 20 feet every 100 years.

Ravenscar is the site of a Roman signal station and of a failed eighteenth-century venture to create a smart resort, doomed by wind and weather. The long coastline stretching south-east to Scarborough is a geologists' delight, while walkers experience something of the loneliness and the extensive views of the moors. The coast is not all suitable for sunbathing or building sand-castles, and so has no camping or caravanning sites, no amusement arcades and few ice-cream carts. Thus the pensive or purposeful are admirably accounted for while the hedonistic can find all the candy-floss they want – as well as a dolphinarium, a vivarium, a medieval castle and an eighteenth-century spa – at the charming resort of Scarborough.

The best approach to Scarborough is to drive in from the south. The road cuts through a chasm in the cliffs across which a footbridge was designed especially as a promenade for visitors in their finery to move between the darkly wooded, landscaped hillside to one of Britain's most magnificent Victorian Gothic seaside hotels. This masterpiece by the designer of Leeds Town Hall, Cuthbert Broderick, was built with 365 rooms, seven floors and four towers – a calendar building, like some of England's stately homes. The road below curves round to follow a

Red roofs of Whitby surround the mouth of the Esk as it meets the North Sea: the historic abbey presides over harbour and town.

wonderfully varied seafront of souvenir shops, cafés, amusement arcades and fish-and-chip shops. A turbanned, oriental figure sits outside his emporium; places of entertainment flash coloured lights that would satisfy Main Street, Las Vegas – and the Bethel Mission Chapel holds its own in brick, with rounded arched windows outlined in a darker shade. At the end of it all is the medieval fishing town, the harbour and piers and lighthouse, and the huge bluff of grey rock on which, 300 feet up, the grey castle sprawls. From here, Marine Drive follows the straight line of almost vertical high cliffs, crowned with villas and hotels, that edge North Beach. The spa that started it all stands at the far end of South Beach under the landscaped hillside, looking a little weather-beaten and advertising anything from ballroom dancing to wrestling. The fine Victorian theatre, recently restored, is as rococo as a seaside theatre should be. At 'Woodend', near the Victorian Museum and Art Gallery, Dame Edith Sitwell and her brother Sacheverell were born. The house keeps memorabilia of the family in the Sitwell Room.

Leaving the high dark moors after Scarborough, the coast follows the morainic ridge that encloses the former Lake of Pickering as far as Filey Brigg, a long ridge of oolitic rock on the seaward side protecting softer rock which has been scoured into caverns and chasms by the rain as well as the waves. Extending a mile into the sea from the foot of North Cliff, most of it is revealed at low tide to form a natural breakwater for the small fishing resort of Filey further south – and a fitting finish, or beginning, for the Cleveland Way. From North Cliff, the walkers are rewarded with a suitably climactic view across Filey Bay to the steep chalk cliffs of the Wolds, and Flamborough Head.

The church of St Mary looks over the Old Harbour at Scarborough. Keel boats and cobles operate from here, landing their catch for auction at the fish market pier.

3 Chalk & Clay

Flamborough Head is almost a region in itself, as rich in history as it is in high cliffs, caves, caverns and seabirds – once known as 'Flamborough Pilots' because their cries warned off ships which until the lighthouse was built in 1806 were lost here with grim regularity. In summer the clifftops flame with gorse and in winter bitter winds scream in from the North Sea. An Iron-Age earthwork, the Danes' Dyke, scores southward from Bempton Cliffs to Sewerby Rocks and almost isolates the nose-like promontory from about two miles west of the head. This busy area supports a golf course and caravan site, tumuli, farms, and the fishing and holiday village of Flamborough with its monument to lost lifeboatmen, its large chapels and its restored church. A gruesome memorial within recalls 'Little Sir Marmaduke' Constable who commanded at Flodden Field at the age of 70 but died, so it is said, when a toad ate out his heart. West of Danes' Dyke, along the southern cliffs, the eighteenth-century mansion Sewerby Hall now houses an art gallery and a museum, and has one room devoted to memorabilia of the pioneer airwoman Amy Johnson who was born in Hull. Just under the arm of the headland is the old fishing port and resort of Bridlington. Flamborough makes a microcosmic introduction to the former East Riding, almost all of which now belongs to Humberside.

North of Flamborough in June, notably along Bempton Cliffs, the ledges are crowded with gannets, razorbills, guillemots, kittiwakes and other seabirds nesting in a raucous mass. The cliffs continue inland and become the Yorkshire Wolds, chalk hills that form the Vale of Pickering's southern edge and then, turning south, contain the eastern limit of the Plain of York. On the eastern side of the ridge between the hills and the sea stretch the clay farmlands, crossed with waterways, known as the Plain of Holderness. The long broad mouth of the mighty Humber makes the south-eastern part of Holderness a peninsula, but since 1981 this isolated piece of Yorkshire has been linked to Lincolnshire and the West Midlands by the world's longest single-span suspension bridge, the Humber Bridge. Yorkshire's only seaport, Kingston-upon-Hull, has grown where the River Hull pours into the Humber. The former capital of the East Riding, Beverley, stands close to the River Hull, and the towers of its superb church Beverley Minster dominate the green flat countryside.

The long, low coastline of Holderness is fast crumbling, but the abruptly curving hook at its tip, Spurn Point, which is a staging post for migratory birds, is growing by longshore drift at the rate of a yard a year. The Wolds were once sea cliffs, and the flat coastal plain was built up by boulder clay and other morainic debris from the Cumbrian and Scandinavian ice sheets. Now the sea is nibbling away at the footpaths, fields, villages and churches which man has dared to place within its reach. The church bell and font of Auburn, sole survivors of a village that had stood at least three miles from the coast in medieval times, are preserved in Wragby Church. Withernsea has lost churches, houses and a pier but Hornsea, halfway along the coast, has shored up its seafront with concrete. Heedless of the historic dangers, holidaymakers can now enjoy a pottery and leisure park, museums and the sandy shore itself, as well as freshwater fishing and sailing on the reedy, bird-haunted waters of Hornsea Mere nearby.

The old fishing port of Bridlington has all the

Opposite Colourful summer at Filey, fishing town turned resort, sheltered by its ridge of oolitic rock which protrudes for a mile into the sea.

fun of the seaside, but it was not a purpose-built resort, and this contributes to its attractions. A commercial fleet of cobles operates, and converted cobles take out fishing parties to catch haddock, cod or plaice. Stones from the old priory are built into the piers of its tidal harbour, and the church that survived the Dissolution, standing away from the sea in the old market town, is thought to be the most magnificent in the old East Riding after Beverley Minster. Across a green, shaded by trees, stands the fourteenth century gatehouse which is now a museum. As in all Yorkshire's villages and towns, Bridlington's history, at times, seems somewhat larger than life. A romantic episode concerns Queen Henrietta Maria who was challenged on landing here with arms and ammunition for her husband Charles I; in a letter she describes how she hid in a ditch while 'the balls sang merrily over our heads, and a sergeant was killed not 20 paces from me. Under this shelter we remained two hours, the bullets flying over us, and sometimes covering us with earth'.

This part of Yorkshire is not a traditional thoroughfare like the Plain of York, nor has it access to the extensive tracts of wilderness or high hill country suitable for recreational pursuits. The rich boulder clay of Holderness, watered by canals, dykes and drains, is intensively and productively cultivated. The gentle sweep of the Wolds is cultivated or grazed but lightly populated, and there are ghosts: the 'lost villages' of Yorkshire that never recovered from the Conqueror's brutal harrying of the North, the fourteenth-century ravages of the Black Death, and later the seizing of arable strips for sheep farming. Yet there is nothing tame about these landscapes. There is drama in their mystery, their village churches are as proud of their rich Romanesque doorways as are those in the West Riding, their grand houses holding treasure and legends, open to the public, reflect local families' long association with the land. Sledmore House in the heart of the Wolds is occupied by a famous East Riding family the Sykes, who over successive generations have contributed to the reclamation of marginal land, the foundation of a famous stud, and the restoration of the churches of the Wolds.

Some way south stands the church that for many surpasses almost any other ecclesiastical building in England, the beautiful Beverley Minster. The construction of the present church began in 1220, the same year as York Minster, and continued over a period of about 200 years in the varying building styles of successive periods which now combine in harmony to follow the Minster's plan of a double cross. The slender majesty of the west front's perpendicular twin towers and the profusion of ornament inside the church contrasts with the flat, water-dominated landscape from which it springs. The exquisite carvings in glowing limestone of the canopy over the Percy tomb, and the rumbustious scenes in the 68 misericords superbly portrayed by the woodcarvers of the Ripon school, equally contrast with the simple slab in the centre of the church where the remains of St John of Beverley are interred. He founded a monastery and church here in about 693 AD and after serving as Archbishop of York from 707 to 718 retired to Beverley where he died and was buried in 721. Although the monastery was destroyed by the Danes, the church came to be venerated. King Athelstan's dagger was laid on the altar before the battle of Brunanburgh at which Athelstan's victory made him king of all England, and Beverley was then made a collegiate and granted the right of sanctuary:

Als Free make I The
As hert may thynke or Egh may see.

John of Beverley was canonised in 1037, and his tomb became a shrine. He had been trained by Hilda of Whitby, and Bede who was his pupil wrote his life story; the Conqueror spared his church. In 1188 a fire destroyed it, and the present beautiful building stands in its place. About half a mile away stands St Mary's Church, hardly less magnificent but quite different in character, begun in the twelfth century as a chapel for the monastery. Here, too, is a wealth of carving, most notably the Beverley Minstrels, a cluster of painted figures around one of the pillars in the nave, and Alice-in-Wonderland's hare, so it is said. The story goes that Lewis Carroll visited Beverley and based his Mad March Hare on this charming carving in another corner of the church.

Another visitor to Beverley was Charles I, whose request to Hull's governor Sir John Hotham that they might dine together that evening had been answered by the plea that the governor 'could not, without betraying the trust committed to him, open the gate to so great a train as his majesty was attended with'. The King ignored this plea and advanced, and in refusing him entry, Hull became the first town to make any overtly hostile gesture in the struggle between

Eroded chalk cliffs of fossil-rich Flamborough Head, where the Yorkshire wolds reach the sea.

Avoiding the drama of Yorkshire's moors or dales the sweeping uplands of the wolds, England's most northerly chalk country, provide fertile farmland and a truly pastoral landscape.

the Crown and Parliament. It was twice unsuccessfully besieged by the Royalists and part of its defence was the flooding of the lands around, to the despair of the country people whose preoccupation was less with who should govern them than with what they might live on. Today, rising from flat Holderness like the noble towers of its village churches, are the cranes and derricks of Hull's docks and the chimney stacks or towers of the industrial lands along the banks of the Humber. Shattered during the Second World War, the third port of England is today a modern town although the ancient 'Old Town' as it is called, situated at the mouth of the river Hull, is being restored. It is already the town's main banking, legal and commercial centre, and has been an important settlement since 1293 when Edward I acquired it as a strategic point of entry on the Humber bank and gave it the title King's Town, or Kingston, granting its Charter in 1299. Hull Trinity House, in the Old Town, is not

merely a handsome Georgian building, but also the headquarters of a 500-year-old guild which has long taken responsibility for the marking and pilotage of the port, for the training of young seamen and care for the old. Trinity House is not generally open to the public; it still has a job to do.

It is the great rivers which meet there that have given Hull her history. And if, by car, you follow the Humber towards its meeting with the combined currents of the Ouse and Wharfe, the Aire and Calder and the Don, you approach the great powerhouse of Yorkshire centred in the cities of South Yorkshire whose growth during the Industrial Revolution helped make Victorian Britain great.

Old-fashioned delicacies at Bridlington Quay, the ancient harbour and port around which a friendly resort has grown.

4 Glass Towers & Marble Halls

In Yorkshire the sweeping administrative changes of 1974 have coincided with an era of urban change in the former West Riding. The new Metropolitan Counties of South and West Yorkshire have set about the clearance of the 'dark Satanic mills', the endless back-to-back housing, and the city centres which grew with nineteenth-century industry. Unfortunately, twentieth-century planning does not always reproduce the same sense of identity or unity, and often improved housing is laid out in soulless patterns, or incongruous traffic plans surround Victorian town halls and other nineteenth-century municipal buildings which stand in their new, pedestrianised (and all-too-often pedestrian) shopping precincts.

South and West Yorkshire make a vital contribution to the nation's economy. While retaining their traditional crafts the towns have been prompted to diversify their industry by present economic realities, and there is keen competition, shared nationally as well as locally, in attracting new firms. The coal and steel-producing towns, notably Sheffield, have always enjoyed easy access to some of England's most strikingly beautiful countryside along the high moors and deep dales of the nearby Pennines. So too have the old wool and textile towns which cling to the steep sides of river valleys – the Aire, the Calder and the Colne – where fast-running, soft water has been necessary for production in all its stages of technological development from the Middle Ages until the present and where the presence of nearby coal measures fuelled the new-fangled machines of the Victorian boom. The museums in these old towns tell the fascinating story of Victorian technology which changed the face of West Riding; parts of the Victorian face remain. For students of urban architecture, exploration in or around the towns of the Industrial Revolution is more rewarding than can be imagined from any brief encounter made by way of motorways that slice through – or close to – their fast-changing hearts.

Sheffield in South Yorkshire has grown among broad hills of the Pennines east of High Peak in Derbyshire. The Rivers Don and Sheaf and their numerous tributaries provided the power that made Sheffield world-famous in the production of cutlery and steel, and Sheffield plate. For centuries, cutlers worked at home in the valleys which now combine within the city's suburbs and distinguished modern centre. Chaucer's 'Sheffield thwitel' would have been made, in one of various centres, from local iron; Flemish settlers brought their craftsmanship in the sixteenth century, and the eighteenth century saw the introduction of steel and plating technology. Factories were built in the valleys during the first half of the nineteenth century, and the third Cutlers' Hall, stately Grecian, went up in 1832, opposite the fifteenth-century Cathedral Church of SS Peter and Paul. With its recently built extension, the church and a continuing sequence of old and new buildings make this determinedly-modern town centre an agreeable place which holds its own against E W Mountford's monumental Town Hall in Pinstone Street. Other parts of modern Sheffield, the parks and shopping areas, the University buildings started in 1905 and continued into the '60s, and the progressive housing projects, have won world-wide acclaim.

The Victorian working towns of Yorkshire are well-endowed with art galleries and museums and with that intriguing, fast-emerging breed the industrial museum. Sheffield's City Museum houses the world's largest collection of Sheffield plate and a unique display of cutlery from the Continent as well as from Sheffield and dating from the sixteenth century. To the south-west of the city, near the remains of Beauchief Abbey, a working museum is based on the eighteenth-century Abbeydale Industrial Hamlet while further north, approaching Barnsley, two historic mills form the focus of a country park laid out round a reservoir. At Cannons Hall in Cawthorne Village just west of the town there is a collection of glass, still an important industry in Barnsley and dating from before the coal seams were worked. Further north at Wakefield, the Charles Waterton Natural History Collection is housed in the former Mechanics' Institute, a dignified Grecian building of the 1820s and precursor of the Victorian ideals of 'self-improvement' for the working man. At Wentworth Terrace the Art Gallery shows sculptures by Barbara Hepworth who was born here in 1903, and by Henry Moore who is a native of nearby Castleford. Wakefield is the county town of the old West Riding and has a coal-based economy although it has been at the heart of the cloth trade since the thirteenth century. A pedestrianised shopping precinct is

dominated by the fifteenth-century cathedral, originally the parish church, whose noble crocketed spire is the tallest in Yorkshire. Not far from this modern town centre is the Town Hall of 1877, whose square grandeur is repeated further along the street in the massive County Hall with its polygonal tower and dome. From an earlier age, and much rebuilt, survives the best of England's four remaining chantry chapels which projects on a bank into the River Calder from a sixteenth-century bridge.

Huddersfield and Halifax like Sheffield are Pennine towns but they are more dramatically sited along the deep slopes of the Colne and the Calder. In all three towns the presence of the gritstone moors is felt close by. These were wool centres in the Middle Ages when the woollen industry was the 'flower and strength and blood and revenue of England', and grew to townships when mills began to be established along the precipitous slopes of the valleys where water and then coal provided a ready source of power. The weavers and clothiers had built their distinctive cottages, with rows of windows along the top storey, close to the moors where they could combine two industries by continuing as sheep farmers. Huddersfield today is renowned not

The Classical portico of the Mappin Art Gallery, in Sheffield's Weston Park, stands almost a mile from the amalgam of Victorian and Futuristic architecture in the City Centre.

only for the production of worsted but also for its Choral Society which sprang from the singing tradition of the non-conformist chapels in these industrial towns. The splendid Italianate Town Hall which rises like a colossus over its modern centre contributed to the Society's success for, like its counterparts, the building was intended not only as a symbol of the town's prestige and wealth and as a temple to hard work, but also as a centre for self-improvement. In this, the concert hall which it contained was intended to play its part. The town's Corinthian-style railway station of the 1840s earns the admiration of Sir Nikolaus Pevsner in his *Buildings of England*, but Pevsner regrets the destruction in 1930 of 'Huddersfield's most famous and historically most important building', its eighteenth-century Cloth Hall whose cupola is preserved in the Tolson Memorial Museum at Ravensknowle Park. Here you can see early weaving apparatus and relics of the Luddite riots. In Lumb Lane at Almondbury are weavers' cottages whose inhabitants, threatened by the introduction of machinery, probably responded to the Luddite cause.

Halifax, like Huddersfield, records local history in museums just outside town. A folk museum is contained in the grounds of Shibden Hall which is an outstanding example of timber-framed building, the earliest part dating from the fifteenth century. The town itself, which is the oldest of the West Riding wool centres, specialised in worsteds and carpet making. Its former prominence as a marketing centre is reflected in the superb Piece Hall, the only example remaining in the region, begun in 1775 for village weavers and clothiers to exhibit their 'pieces' of cloth for sale. The building is brought to life by the installation of craft-, antique- and bookshops in the colonnaded merchants' galleries, and a cheerfully domestic weekly market is conducted on the grassed and cobbled quadrangle. Halifax still retains its Victorian centre, and seems less fragmented than its neighbours. Sir Charles Barry's town hall and the fine Civic Theatre (spoiled by unsympathetic signwriting) have benefited by an extensive cleaning programme, but the fifteenth-century church of St John where cloth trading once took place in the porch stands too far down in the valley for the stone-scouring machines to manage the slope, and the church's blackened façade remains, like the grandiloquent Victorian town halls, a monument to the region's hard-won prosperity.

Two or three miles up-river stands picturesque Heptonstall where weavers' cottages twist along a moorland ridge, and worship still takes place in the world's longest continuously used Wesleyan chapel. In the deep valley are the mills and terraces of Hebden Bridge which developed with the introduction of steam power. Clothing manufacture is still an important part of the area's industry, while only three miles away is the local beauty spot Hardcastle Crags, where the Calder rushes over rocks under a canopy of trees.

In 1858 Queen Victoria, opening the magnificent Leeds Town Hall, described the city as 'a stirring and thriving seat of English Industry embellished by an edifice not inferior to those stately piles which still attest to the ancient opulence of the commercial centres of Italy and Flanders'. Just over a century later, Leeds was proclaiming itself 'The Motorway City of the Seventies'. In the last decade or so, as a university town and one of England's most important commercial centres, and anxious to attract new industry, the town has swept aside many proud symbols of past achievements along with its 'mean streets' and has replaced them with tower blocks and motorways. Sightseers on wheels, following the one-way system, gain an encapsulated view of Leeds' former gracious grandeur reflected in Cuthbert Broderick's impressive and confident buildings as they flash past. The dome of Broderick's immense, imposing Town Hall still dominates; his fine elliptical Corn Exchange remains, while his Mechanics' Institute advertising its new rôle as Civic Theatre in pink neon cheerfully merges the old order with the new. The Civic Hall of 1935, classical, and with slim turrets topped by owls, bridges the gap between Italy or Flanders and pre-war Britain. In the industrial heart of the city by the river or the canal are old brick warehouses and mills, while a rather run-down quarter hides Marshall's Flax Mill of about 1840, built to represent an Egyptian temple and equipped with underfloor heating, and a roof-garden with sheep grazing it for the comfort and benefit of the workers. Now it is in a decrepit state, like much of this interesting area. For pedestrians this spacious, hilly and energetic city has many attractive corners locked into the one-way system, among them the covered shopping arcades of Victorian iron and glass, high and light and generously ornamented, and still performing the function for which they were planned; or the Town Hall's interior which is as awe-inspiring as its masterful outward bulk. The lofty and ornate Victoria Hall, it is said, can stage anything bar a circus – although in Victoria's day the very idea would have been beyond the pale. Blondin himself had requested permission to walk the tightrope across the Victoria Hall, and had been refused. The Victorians built an exceptional concert hall, however, with the requisite mighty organ, and the Leeds International Pianoforte Competition has been held here trianually since 1963. Further out, patches of Georgian and Victorian residential areas are besieged by new housing schemes and vacant ground, through which the arterial road system carries us with ease to other places of interest nearby.

Harewood House, the home of the Earl and Countess of Harewood, is close enough to provide Leeds families with pleasant afternoon outings in beautiful parkland, surrounded by the rolling countryside which borders the Plain of York. The real attractions of Harewood are John Carr's grand classical façades, of which the south was remodelled by Sir Charles Barry in 1843 –when an Italianate terrace was added to Capability Brown's landscaping – and the inspired interiors of Robert Adam. Adam achieved his hallmark of elegant harmony by commissioning the interior decorations from great artists and craftsmen of the day, including Angelica Kauffman and Thomas Chippendale. Each piece of mastery in moulding, carving, wall painting and furniture seems to have been created solely as a proper setting for the next.

Close to Leeds, on its western edge, Temple Newsam House has in its grounds two golf-courses and an open-cast coal mine. Sadly, as at Harewood House, recent storms have devastated much woodland. The impressive Jacobean-styled building stands on a terrace divorced from the grounds and has a severe appearance. The present layout has changed little externally since alterations were carried out in 1630 by the financier Sir Arthur Ingram who bought the house from James I's impecunious cousin Ludovick, Duke of Lennox. Ingram raised an arresting inscription around the roof praising the Holy Trinity and calling for peace and goodwill, which ends 'HONOUR AND TRUE ALLEGIANCE TO OUR GRACIOUS KING; LOVING AFFECTION AMONG HIS SUBJECTS; HEALTH AND PLENTY BE WITHIN THIS HOUSE'. Within this house today, a museum administered by the owners, Leeds Corporation, holds a treasury of paintings and furniture collected from all over the world

and set out to reflect changing styles from period to period. Twentieth-century paintings and sculpture are included, and there are displays of Leeds pottery. Leeds University works closely with the museum staff on its programme of research and education. Advanced techniques of restoration have effected some miraculous restoration of mouldings and plasterwork, notably in the dramatic and beautiful Long Gallery, where furniture from the house itself is displayed.

Students and university professors are among those who live in the handsome Victorian suburb of Headingley, just north-west of the city centre, which is a place of pilgrimage for Yorkshiremen as the site of one of England's four Test cricket grounds. Cricket commentaries from Headingley constantly refer to 'the Kirkstall Lane end' but few people outside Yorkshire know the great abbey to which it refers. Along the main Ilkley road its blackened spectral ruin appears from behind a bank of trees, and closer inspection reveals a surrounding park of lawns and trees where the monastic ruins spread to the River Aire. Kirkstall did not prosper and develop as richly as other

Cistercian houses and its gritstone walls, the loftiest remains of England's ruined abbeys, illustrate clearly the austere spirituality of the twelfth-century Cistercians. The great gatehouse survived the Dissolution as a private house and is now a well-known folk museum whose displays include 'The Streets', a collection of buildings rescued from the redevelopment of central Leeds.

It has been suggested that Bradford Town Hall was built in retaliation for Leeds Town Hall, which had emulated (and overshadowed) Bradford's St George's Hall. Famed for its acoustics, St George's in its heyday featured Paderewski and Patti as well as the Two Headed Nightingale and General Tom Thumb, and Gertie Millar the Gaiety Girl – also a Bradford girl. Recently, St George's has been restored to music after serving as a cinema. The Town Hall is a Victorian Gothic building with an ecclesiastical air and a fine campanile which was likened to an exploding rocket when it first appeared. Faced with local stone it stands at one end of Market Street, which has at the other end the earlier Venetian Gothic Bradford Exchange. With the

The town hall to end all town halls, a superb example of the Classic Revival, created for Leeds by Cuthbert Broderick in the 1850s.

patron saint of woolcombers, St Blaise, looking down from the tower, this looks even more like a church: it was a temple to trade, where transactions once opened and closed with a handshake. 'It is probably true', proclaimed the Bradford Chamber of Commerce in its centenary copy of 1951, 'that there is not a type of wool grown anywhere in the world...for which a buyer cannot be found on the Bradford Exchange. It has aptly been described as the hub of the wool trade of the world'. Thirty years later the Bradford Exchange houses offices and market stalls, and the columns of the Alhambra Theatre portico face the reflecting glass of the Metropolitan Police Headquarters, in the centre of a city which is energetically seeking replacements for its former industry. While Leeds stands close to the open green Plain of York, Bradford with its Moravian, German and Asian settlements is within the reach of the wild moors that the Bradford-born composer Frederick Delius loved, and the Brontës knew so well. J B Priestley was born in Bradford; David Hockney's work hangs in the Art Gallery of his home town. The city's past as the greatest of the Victorian wool towns lives in the Industrial Museum at Moorside Road, Eccleshill, where a former spinning mill is put through its paces at advertised times. At nearby Bingley the Five Rise Locks on the Leeds and Liverpool Canal, a major engineering achievement of the eighteenth century, are still worked for pleasure boats, and near Shipley is one of the earliest examples of industrial planning in the north, the mill town Saltaire. Cathedral-like, the mill crouches in the deep valley by the river, flanked by trees and grass in Roberts Park and faced by the beautiful domed tower and portico of the Congregational Church. Down the steep slope of the valley march terraces of workers' cottages, with arched windows, in dark stone. This pioneering development which included a Library and Institute was the work of Sir Titus Salt, who named the streets after Victoria and Albert, himself, his wife Caroline and other members of his family. Established in an age before planning became a public responsibility, Saltaire is seen in the interesting perspective of post-war housing estates between the towns.

Old and new in Bradford City Centre: the recently cleaned Victorian Gothic town hall, and the footbridge approach to Bradford's Travel Interchange.

5 The Wild Dales

Haworth makes a good introduction to the northern dales from the industrial south, for the steep cobbled street leading to the Brontë sisters' parsonage overlooks a huddle of mills far below in the valley, while the dark church and the sloping churchyard with its large and ornate and blackened tombstones listing at all angles under tall trees and harsh rooks' cries – and the parsonage at the top – are set against the wild moorland's edge. Here the Brontë sisters spent many childhood hours that live in their writing, whether in their impassioned novels, or Charlotte's lines that

> Speak of the North! A lonely moor
> Silent and dark and trackless swells,
> The waves of some wild streamlet pour
> Hurriedly through its ferny dells.

Three miles south-west of Haworth, just below Withins Heights, is the ruin of a farm which may have been the home of the Earnshaws, the 'Wuthering Heights' of Emily Brontë's novel in which the writer makes the presence of the moors felt even inside the house:

The fire had smouldered to ashes; the room was filled with the damp, mild air of the cloudy evening; and so still, that not only the murmur of the beck down Gimmerton was distinguishable, but its ripples and its gurgling over the pebbles, or through the large stones which it could not cover.

The dark, dour buildings of Haworth climbing up from the depths of its industrialised dale make sharp contrast with the natural wilderness beyond. It is supplemented rather than swamped by the smartly painted craft studios, continuing the textile tradition, and the souvenir shops inevitable in a site of literary pilgrimage. In the parsonage at the top of the town, personal relics of the Brontës make their story seem all the more poignant, set out as they are in the small rooms where they lived and worked and in the museum annexe at the back of the house, all now open to the public gaze. The saturnine moors beyond the parsonage window seem utterly unchanged.

The misnamed 'Pennine Chain', which extends from Derbyshire to Scotland, is a survival of a long plateau scored by rivers and ice-age glaciers. The hills and valleys that formed part of Yorkshire's West and North Ridings occupy almost all of the central Pennines. Most rivers flow east or south-east, and the best-known dales between the industrialised South's Airedale and wild Upper Teesdale are Wharfedale, Nidderdale, Wensleydale and Swaledale. Where lesser streams – becks – join the upper reaches of these dales, remote and wild valleys score deep into the heart of the Pennine system. Generally the higher peaks of the region are characterised by long moorland ridges, topped by rocky outcrops, which plunge to the rivers in their deep dales. In some parts the ridges' steep slopes have been scoured by glaciers so that they look like an inverted rib-cage. This is carpeted with brownish-green pasture and divided by drystone walls into a patchwork of small squares or strips which can sometimes follow medieval, Saxon or even Celtic plans. The tamed English word 'dale', from the Norse *dalr*, may not prepare a stranger for the wheeling, crying peewits, black-faced sheep, stone outbarns built into the sides of the hills, and remote villages built of gritstone. Each dale has its own character, and in those areas where limestone predominates the fantastic landscape attracts many visitors from the hard-working South Yorkshire towns, as well as from further afield. This is country to see on foot, and it is

The familiar outline of Pen-y-Ghent's grey, hard cap of millstone grit broods over pleasant limestone country in Ribblesdale.

traversed by the oldest and longest of Britain's long-distance footpaths, the Pennine Way. On the many footpaths and tracks we follow in the footsteps of Celtic tribes, of monastic shepherds and miners, of pack-trains and pedlars going to market, and of funeral processions to hilltop barrows or later churchyards. Between these old routes and the ramblers' planned walks, and the modern roads which cars can pass, are the farms, villages and towns where only recently tourism has taken the place of traditional industries like mining, horse breeding or knitting – and which seem yet unchanged.

Some of Yorkshire's most striking Pennine scenery is seen in the limestone district around Ribblesdale. The river rises in the county's western Pennines and flows southwards, passing Whernside which at 2419 feet is the highest of West Yorkshire's gritstone-capped 'Three Peaks'. The others, Ingleborough Hill and Pen-y-Ghent, are separated by the Ribble as it flows on its course for Lancashire and the Irish Sea. Looking

like crouching beasts, the long dark profiles of these peaks dominate the fresh green pastures and light-coloured stone walls of the lower, limestone country, and are the haunt of climbers, hikers, geologists and pot-holers. On Ingleborough Hill are some fine examples of 'swallow holes' where streams tumbling down from the millstone grit reach the porous limestone and disappear into the hillside, to reappear further down where the limestone ends, or reaches saturation point. One of the best-known, Gaping Ghyll, is a shaft 350 feet deep dropping to a great cavern where England's highest known waterfall plunges from an underground waterway. The fantastic scenery extends eastward along the road from Ingleton to Settle, where the road runs alongside Giggleswick Scar, a great limestone cliff which was formed when earth-folding created the multiple Craven Faults along this part of the Pennines. Still eastward in Malhamdale, whence the productive Aire springs, is West Yorkshire's

biggest lake Malham Tarn which is contained within morainic debris from the last Ice Age. The Aire once flowed from here to fall 300 feet over the craggy precipice known as Malham Cove, but the water has seeped down and now issues from several miles further along Malhamdale. A sister stream rising beneath Malham's sheer whitish cliff flows between drystone walls, grass and trees, and past ancient field systems to meet the Aire. The level clifftop of Malham Cove is formed of limestone pavement, a stone platform dissected by deep cracks called grykes in which the rich soil supports woodland plants such as bluebells and wood anemones. Equally striking landscape can be seen just to the north at Gordale Scar where a river has repeatedly dissolved and undermined its limestone bed, leaving the deep gorge dry and following a yet deeper course underground.

The Ingleborough-Settle road, the A65, crosses Airedale at Skipton and Wharfedale at the spa town Ilkley, just north of the moor of *baht 'at*

fame. From here a road follows the Wharfe's course toward Kilnsey Crag, Kettlewell and the steep dales of its upper reaches. Just north of Ilkley, near the road,

> The stately priory was reared;
> And Wharfe as he moved along
> To Matins joined a mournful voice,
> Nor failed at Evensong.

Bolton Priory, often miscalled Bolton Abbey, still celebrates Matins and Evensong, for today it is a parish church contained in the soaring nave of what was once an Augustinian house. Set in a green and pastoral landscape, the ruins of the monastic buildings at the east end are in the course of preservation but a beautiful scale model made by local school children is

For visitors to Yorkshire's Pennines, Gordale Scar in Malhamdale forms an exciting part of this region's phenomenal limestone landscape.

55

A hill farm in Wharfedale. From its stony beginnings in wild Langstrothdale, the River Wharfe flows through hill-farming country and then encounters increasingly pastoral scenery.

displayed in the church. Wordsworth's poem tells about the legendary founding of the priory by the grieving mother of a boy who drowned as he attempted to leap the Strid – a narrow chasm about two miles up-river where the waters squeeze through a gap one yard wide and 30 feet deep. The foaming chaos of water and rock makes a splendid spectacle but a dangerous one, for the river here is deep and the undercurrents are strong. This is uncharacteristic landscape for lower Wharfedale, whose valley is wide enough to accommodate a popular road leading from Ilkley past Bolton Priory and the Strid through meadowlands, woods and quiet villages until the climbers' delight Kilnsey Crag is passed, when the road begins to climb into wilder, barer country around Kettlewell. A Youth Hostel here is a meeting-place for climbers and pot-holers, who

look somewhat incongruous in their gear among the stone cottages and steep streets of this old town. The Wharfe comes down from the north-west and just to the north-east, flanking Coverdale, is the dark *couchant* bulk of Great Whernside, perversely 100 feet lower than Whernside of the 'Three Peaks' although considerably greater than Little Whernside which crouches a little further along the dale. From these heights spring the beginnings of the River Nidd.

Nidderdale in its lonely upper reaches flows through a series of reservoirs, built early this century, haunted by wildfowl and bird watchers. Further down-river the limestone scenery again attracts visitors, notably to How Stean Beck and its cavern-lined gorge, or Stump Cross Caverns on Greenhow Hill, discovered by miners in 1860 and now a fairyland (fairy-lit) of exotically-named galleries and formations. Just as fantastically named – and formed – are the rock formations known as Brimham Rocks, near Pateley Bridge. Covering high heather moors, these great boulders of millstone grit have been weathered to assume the shapes from which they are named: *Dancing Bear, Druid's Skull, Baboon.* Their grotesque shapes gaze from their heights across Nidderdale to the Plain of York. The river flows across the plain to meet the Ouse, passing Ripley Castle where Lady Ingilby against her will put up Oliver Cromwell after his victory at Marston Moor from which her Royalist husband and sister-in-law were yet to return. The lady and the soldier spent a wakeful night, seated, she with a pistol in her hand. The castle was largely rebuilt in 1780 but in the Knight's Chamber with its well-preserved wagon roof remains the carved oak inscription:

> Better is poverty with mirth and gladness
> Than riches with sorrow and sadness.

Following the north-bound road to Ripon and then turning west brings travellers to a pleasant road which introduces Wensleydale, the Valley of the Ure. The country is tawny-green, and hawthorn hedges bouncing over the contours enclose arable or grazing land. Handsome market towns stand by the rivers. One of the first is Masham, pronounced 'Mazm', which for centuries was one of northern England's most important sheep markets. The church whose spire can be seen rising among trees from the market place stands on a Saxon site, and a carved shaft is preserved in the churchyard. Theakston's Breweries behind the market square produce 'Old Peculier' – one of England's most celebrated traditional beers.

The monks of Jervaulx Abbey, which was built further along the dale, introduced Wensleydale cheese. The haunting remains of this Cistercian house, founded in 1156, are reached by a rough footpath from the road. Half-hidden by trees, the ruins are enclosed by dry-stone walls whose stones, forming a herring-bone pattern, have come from the fallen abbey. The owners have allowed the natural grasses and flowers of the pasturelands to adorn but not possess the ruined works of man. Purple rock plants grow from the few lofty façades and the heaps of fallen arches or pillars lie among ivy and fern. The capitals of the octagonal pillars in the aisles of the chapter house have their own foliage of stone. Many of the dressed stones show masons' marks, and there are a number of worn figures and tombs among the ruins, which have a clear ground plan. The practical visitor will want to chart the layout of the church and monastic buildings, the romantic can wander through grass and trees and let the past seep in.

The road rolling through Wensleydale continues the feeling of rubbing shoulders with the past. This is settled country, but never tame. The village of East Witton seems inexplicably laid out – a long rectangle of stone cottages set around rough grass with a large boulder at the far end and the church facing the green from across the road. At Middleham, where the monks of Jervaulx are said to have introduced the local industry of horse breeding, a grey castle ruin stands above the sloping town, the looming façades constructed from immense blocks of gritstone. Once known as 'the Windsor of the North', this dominating edifice for a time was occupied by Warwick the King Maker, who with his retinue was said to consume half-a-dozen oxen at breakfast. The southern end of the castle, now levelled, shows the remains of a vast circular oven, and next to it a horse-mill.

As forbidding as Middleham Castle, and with four towers still standing, Bolton Castle commands Wensleydale from its northern slopes a few miles further along. The fourteenth-century castle was built by Richard, the first Lord Scrope, and for three centuries hereafter this important family lived here in state. The builders sought to combine comfort with strength, in those days a novel idea, and they included ingenious designs which caused remark by Leland in the sixteenth century: 'chimneys were conveyed by tunnils made in the syde of the walls, betwixt the lights in the haull. And by this means, and by no covers, is the smoke of the hearthe in the haull wonder strangely conveyed'. In the same century Mary Queen of Scots was detained here with a vast retinue, half of whom had to be lodged in the village. She was allowed to ride over these hills with her numerous companions for exercise; she tried to escape and was recaptured along Leyburn Shawl, a scenic terrace of oak and sycamore and fir giving panoramic views along a limestone ridge between the village of Preston and the important market town of Leyburn. Her romantic intriguing with Lady Scrope's brother the Duke of Norfolk was to cost the Duke his head. Mary's rooms can be seen in one of the towers, and enough of this well-preserved ruin remains to house a restaurant and the Wensleydale Folk Museum.

The main road following Wensleydale along its south bank passes through the quiet village of Wensley, once important enough to give the dale its name, *en route* to a romantic and well-known beauty spot, the Aysgarth Force, where the river plunges between high wooded banks down a series of waterfalls. A striking viewpoint is gained from the sixteenth-century bridge whose single span of 70 feet commands the Upper Falls and links the south and north bank roads as they follow the river westward into the heart of the Pennines. The country gets wilder and lonelier as the roads pass villages like Askrigg, once known for knitting, brewing, clock-making and bull-baiting, or Bainbridge where the Romans held a fort, and where the Wensleydale horn has been blown to guide travellers since William the Conqueror owned the forest that once covered the bare moors. The Romans built a road from here to Lancaster. Climbing straight as an arrow south-west across the moors to Ingleborough, the road forms part of the Pennine Way which has followed up hill and down dale from Malham to arrive at upper Wensleydale's chief market town, Hawes.

Hawes has an important livestock market and a Wensleydale cheese factory. In Station Yard is the Upper Dales Folk Museum, run by Yorkshire's social chroniclers of the present century, Marie Hartley and Jean Ingilby. Another attraction open to the public is the 200-foot waterfall, and in Victorian times the ravine's acoustics drew brass bands here to hold their annual contests, besides other events. Best of all, surely, must have been the feat performed by Blondin who walked the heights by tightrope pausing to cook an omelette halfway across.

A road leads northward from Hawes between Lovely Seat and Great Shunnor Fell across Buttertubs Pass out of gentle, broad Wensleydale into steep-sided Swaledale. Wild country, it is much-visited in summer and dangerous in winter. The 'buttertubs' on the grass-covered cliffs are another phenomenon of limestone country – deep hollows eroded by water, in which rowan trees and ferns grow. Most are situated on the west of the road which is one of the country's highest, giving breathtaking views of hills and more hills between the dales. Immediately below at the foot of Kisdon are the hamlets of Muker and Thwaite, the home and inspiration of the pioneer nature

Set amid meadowlands of the River Wharfe, Bolton Priory was founded by Alicia de Romilly in 1151.

Hebden village, by the River Wharfe: nearby are Hebden Gill and the fantastic Stump Cross Caverns toward Pateley Bridge.

Opposite Not Arizona but North Yorkshire's Brimham Rocks, grotesque eroded stones of millstone grit covering about 60 square miles of heather moorland.

61

photographer Cherry Kearton and his writer
brother Richard whose books Cherry illustrated at
the beginning of his career. Muker has an annual
sheep – or 'tup' – sale, and this is real sheep
country with its own hardy breed of curly-horned
sheep with grey and black heads. The steep sides
of the valley are lonely and exposed, the walls
march over the bare contours and here you see the
lone two-storey outbarns for sheltering livestock
and hay miles from home, typical Norse
husbandry, although the buildings are no older
than 200 years old. All along here, too, are disused
mines. So the gaunt and tawny moors continue
eastward to Reeth, one-time mining capital of the
dale. From here the landscape softens to pastures
and trees with brown moorland peaks along the
high ridges of the dale, as the Swale flows toward
the Plain of York and to Richmond, which for many
Yorkshire people, north, south, east or west, is
Yorkshire's finest town.

It must have been pleasant after a hard journey
along the Old North Road or over the dales to
arrive at the sloping, spacious market square
curved round the castle yard, with room for the
church and some shops in the centre. In 1771 a
large obelisk was erected opposite the church,
and the Town Hall which stands among Georgian
and Victorian buildings around the southern side
of the square was built in 1756, predating those of
the industrial south by about 100 years. The
awesome castle that Alan Rufus began five years
after the Conquest on an almost perpendicular
outcrop of rock beside the River Swale was one of
the first of the Norman fortresses to have been
built. From the castle's battlemented top, 100 feet
up, this fine town with its Georgian streets and
wynds, the Swale and the moors, can be taken in
at a glance. The castle's curtain walls date from
the eleventh century and the immense keep,
built over the gatehouse, dates from the twelfth
when market stalls first appeared. Outliving the
castle, the market still finds room for stalls on its
uneven cobbled ground. Over the years its
customers would have included Franciscan friars
whose monastery has left a fine tower, and later
perhaps Frances I'Anson, the 'sweet lass of
Richmond Hill'. Certainly she visited the Theatre
Royal in Friars Wynd, for she attended its opening
in 1778 with her brother, then Richmond's mayor.
The theatre closed 60 years later, and after many

Deep in woodland,
Aysgarth Force cascades
over a series of limestone
ridges along a
spectacular half-mile of
the River Ure in
Wensleydale.

ignominious rôles – including corn store and salvage depot – its stepped pit and raised stage were recognised in 1940 as the hallmarks of a Georgian theatre, one of two from this period remaining in Britain. The theatre was reopened in 1962 to the strains of the famous song which declares,

> I'd crowns resign to call thee mine
> Sweet lass of Richmond Hill.

Not far from this beguiling town the Romans' major road crosses the Tees into Durham at Piercebridge. Since the boundary changes of 1974 the turbulent beauty of higher Teesdale has been awarded to Co. Durham, including the mining town Middleton-in-Teesdale which now serves as a touring base without removing its workaday face. This is a spectacular region, containing Mickle Fell, once the highest hill in Yorkshire at 3696 feet; Cauldron Snout where, depending on the elements, the Tees trickles or hurtles over block-like ledges of dark basalt; High Force where after a six-mile journey from the Snout the Tees divides and thunders over a 70-foot cliff, once felicitously separating the two counties so that the roar and misty spume of the falls belonged to both.

Perhaps if you have walked the Pennine Way (which turns westward towards Cumbria at Cauldron Snout) it does not matter whether this waterfall or that summit belongs to Yorkshire or Durham. The journey through the Yorkshire dales by this time will be a complete and unique experience. The singularity of the Yorkshireman and the county he knows to be his home is not to be changed by the stroke of a pen, at least not for decades thereafter, for the character of Yorkshire has been built over centuries and over the ages.

Richmond: a medieval church, a Georgian and Victorian market place and the moors of Swaledale beyond, viewed from the mighty castle around which this handsome town grew.